Be the Cool Kid in High School

Ryan Sand

Be the Cool Kid in High School
2nd Edition, published May 30th 2016

Other titles by the author:

Solid: A Guide to Gain Confidence and Get Rid of Insecurity

Contents

Foreword

This is not a high school *survival* guide. This is a guide for success. For taking the pop-culture monster called high school and making it your bitch.

This book isn't for everyone. Why? First of all, I'm a man. I don't have experience of what high school is like for a girl, so I can't really advise the ladies on that. Maybe I'll write a book with my sister someday, but the point is that this book wasn't written with the ladies in mind. Although the advice in it can be applied regardless of gender, I don't talk about the unique issues that young women experience.

This book also isn't really for the people who are already great at high school. The popular kids, the ultra-sociable ones, the star athletes. They might learn a few useful things from this book, maybe a lot, but they usually have enough luck, natural gifts, and social skills to just be good at high school naturally.

No, this book is for people with untapped potential who aren't sure *how* to tap it. And I don't need to tell you that you are filled with untapped potential. Most of us are. It's a shame that the majority of us grow old without finding out just what we can achieve. In this book, I've outlined some of the most important things that you need to do to take advantage of your time and youth and make the next few years of your life a success.

My advice is based on the things that I have been through myself, from high school, through college and adult life. If the content in this book is short, rest assured, it's because I have decided not to fill it with junk. You won't find cartoons, jokes, or diagrams in it. I'm not trying to fool you with charts and colors.

This book is all straight talk without any fluff and without any sugarcoating either. It's the book I wish someone would have written for me. A "Cliff Notes" on what matters most – well, aside from the education. I'm going to leave the academics for someone else to teach you (at least for now. But don't be surprised if I come up with a guide for study habits and what **not** to do!)

High expectations yet? Let me take them down a peg. This book will not make you the *coolest* kid in high school. That probably is not going to happen, at least, not unless you are dedicated, blessed, and born under a fortunate star. Regardless of what society will tell you, most of the successful people are gifted with it. It's like an angel visited them when they were still in the cradle and blessed them with good fortune. Good looks, good luck, good teeth, you get the idea?

What this book *will* do is give you the opportunity to look at things through a new perspective, because at some point in life, the kid gloves *are* going to come off. The sooner the better, if you ask me. With enough planning, discipline, and dedication, you can join the ranks of the people who *did* achieve success by working hard.

One last point. The ideas and suggestions that I cover in my writing can be applied throughout life. There is nothing that is limited to "high school". Whether it is about having confidence in yourself, or how you get that confidence, both of these are things that you will need at some point or another. The importance of maintaining great hygiene and personal affect? Essential throughout your life. Understanding that humans in a pack-like hierarchy will always try to one-up you, or the fact that bullying does not end on your graduation day are other lessons that you need to learn. You may encounter bullies at a supermarket or in your future job. So as I said before, you need to learn some things, and the sooner you learn them, the better…

BUT

I do have to point out something. Life doesn't have to be about popularity. Strong relationships and networking are things that *will* help you throughout your life, so you should develop your social skills. But if you try too hard to have people like you, that's actually a turn-off. Hell, maybe you don't care whether people like you or not! As long as you decide what's important to you, set goals, and work towards them, that's all that really matters.

The advice in this book isn't given to you *just* so you can find ways to make other people like you. If you're a good person with decent manners, people will probably like you. People probably like you already. The advice in this book is meant to give you the insight and knowledge to make less mistakes. To do more things successfully. So take my advice and do things right the first time.

About the Author

I'm Ryan Sand, the second of four kids. I graduated with a bachelor's degree in business, but I always wanted to be a writer. I enjoyed reading novels more than anything and if you'd asked me if I would be writing a *self-help* book for high school kids when I was *in* high school I probably would have thought about it for a bit and said "nah". That's because I didn't have any advice for you back then.

I was just your Average Joe in high school. I had plenty of friends and no enemies (well, just about. It's kind of hard to have *no* enemies). I've been bullied a few times here and there, so I know what it feels like. I wasn't a jock and I didn't belong in any cliques or groups. Not the worst way to go through high school, but it also wasn't the best. My parents had relationship troubles while I was in grade school and divorced right before my freshman year, so I also know what it's like to go through school while experiencing a rough home life, though I have to thank my parents for doing the best they could. They couldn't get along, but they tried (unsuccessfully) to prevent that from negatively affecting us.

I wrote this book because I wanted to give the other Average Joes the advice that no one gave me. Think of it as a manual with all the basics that you need to know about having a successful experience in high school and most of the advice will take you through college as well, with a little tweaking here and there.

I've divided the book up into three main parts: The **Mental**, the **Physical**, and the **Social**. At the end of the book, there is a section that wraps up some odds and ends that I didn't fit into the first three sections. If you enjoy this book, I'm glad. I wasn't joking when I said that I wish someone had written something just like this and given it to *me* when I hit puberty.

Go ahead and recommend it to a friend.

Follow me on Facebook at:

www.facebook.com/RyanSandBlog

or email me at:

ryan.sand.hs@hotmail.com

Chapter One: Mental

Psychology: *It's All in The Mind*

To withstand the harsh battleground that is called life, you will need to master the mind. When we talk about psychology, usually we're talking about the way that people think. What they think, why they think, how they think— you get the idea.

That is the psychology of people around you and something I will talk about shortly. But before that, you have to realize that your own psychology is just as important. Even more important. In order to do well in high school, to do well throughout **life**, you are going to need to develop your mind. Your mental toughness. Your resistance to stress and to the influence of others.

If you don't have a strong mental center, you will be manipulated. People will be taking advantage of you. You won't have the **courage** to stick up for yourself when you need to stick up for yourself.

See, this is something about life that you might have been told before, or maybe not, but the only person you have to depend on is yourself. Sure, your family might help you. Sure you have friends. But at the end of the day, it is always just you against the world. You should not expect the assistance of others.

For this reason, it is crucial that you develop the ability and skills to stand up for yourself and to speak up for yourself. To have your own voice and opinion. To be honest about your weaknesses and strengths. Because it will be from that strong center in you that you find the motivation and strength to do the things that you want to do in life.

What is at the core of having a strong psyche? Of being mentally strong? **Confidence**. A genuine belief in yourself and your abilities and worth. Confidence isn't something that you can just buy and put on (actually, you can, but it takes a LOT of money to *buy* confidence). It's something that you develop from getting experience, skills, and knowledge. It comes from knowing your strengths and weaknesses. You will see many ways in which you can increase your confidence in the coming chapters, just remember: **confidence is the key to everything you accomplish.**

Pack Mentality: *Chimps in Brand Name Clothing*

Human beings are pack animals. Actually, more like troop animals. We aren't like wolves in a pack. We're more like chimpanzees in a troop. Have you ever seen a chimpanzee in person? Go online, look them up. You'll probably find as many videos of chimpanzees being nice as there are of them being cruel, merciless jerks.

Look up wolves. They're nice. When they aren't killing something for food or fighting over territory, they are just beautiful. They're majestic and family-oriented. No, humans aren't wolves. We're chimps, and it is through that stark analogy that we will understand the troop mentality of high school kids and society in general.

Primate life is structured in a hierarchy, like the levels of a ladder, and the bottom rung is the last place you want to be. People are cruel and petty by nature; they just learn to hide it as they grow older (though some people really *are* nice). Many kids will try to find their place in the social hierarchy by "feeling it out". Who can they ridicule and insult? Well, that person is must be beneath them. Who is off-limits, either too big or too popular for them to insult without suffering a backlash? Well, that person must be above them.

The French philosopher Voltaire wrote, in a quote that is often misattributed:

To determine the true rulers of any society, all you must do is ask yourself this question: Who is it that I am not permitted to criticize?

Look at the social hierarchy the same as Voltaire did, and you will have an idea of who is "in charge". When they start out, some individuals will try to find their place in the social hierarchy directly, by testing their limits. They will be looking to make friends and also, incidentally, making enemies when they try to put others down.

But how does this relate to you? Well, you are going to use this chimpanzee theory and apply it in your social interactions. Here are some basic tenets for how to deal with others:

Don't be a pushover. This is easier said than done, but it's also not complicated. Do not let yourself be put down by anyone (if you can help it). Especially when it is people that you *know* are not high on the social ladder. Ironically, the lower someone is on the social ladder, the more likely they are to go around looking for someone else to bully. But now you know why they are doing it and you know that you should NOT let them. But how do you deal with it?

There are several ways to deal with bullying and aggression. By the time you are through with this book, you should have the confidence and self-knowledge to know what approaches are best for you and a fair idea of some good ways to deal with bullying.

Don't be aggressive in your normal interactions. Nobody likes a person who goes around being bossy and trying to tell everyone what to do. Unless you are the top chimp, you can't go around telling people what to do. Instead, look at people as your equals. Be kind, be friendly, but understand your limits and boundaries. Don't let anyone step on your toes and don't go stepping on the toes of others.

Set your boundaries. Setting boundaries is a part of learning how to say no and when to put your foot down. It's the balance you need to find between the two points listed above. The balance between not being too pushy and not being a pushover.

You need to understand how to draw boundaries between yourself and others. This can be in terms of physical boundaries, or emotional boundaries. Regardless of which one it is, it's important to be able to draw a line between the things that are okay and those that aren't.

If someone is roughing you up and getting physical with you when you aren't okay with it, you need to learn to draw the line. To make it clear that play-fighting and wrestling hijinks aren't welcome.

But take into consideration that some guys may be good-natured about this. Sure, the chimpanzee part of them may be trying to assert some kind of superiority, but if you are actually friends with someone who has these physical tendencies (assuming he or she is not physically *attracted* to you) you can be more understanding and friendlier about drawing boundaries. It all depends on you and your school policies about violence. But don't overreact in a situation that doesn't require it.

Humiliation

When it comes to people's fears, humiliation is top of the list, even higher than being beaten up or hurt. Physical injury is bad, but humiliation cuts right down to your ego: what you see yourself as deep inside.

Almost all of us have this humongous fear of humiliation and with this understanding, many people (bullies) *will* try to humiliate you. They may see it as the easiest way to cut you down. What you **need** to learn, though, is that humiliation is easily blown away by confidence. If you genuinely don't care about something that may humiliate you (a typical example might be that you accidentally farted in class), people cannot use it to make fun of you. Just shrug your shoulders and say "it's cool, man. It could happen to anybody."

No matter how humiliating something is, there's almost nothing that can stand in the way of confidence and a genuine lack of concern. Joke about it, blow it, off, whatever it is. Understand that the only thing that makes humiliation effective is that you *let it affect you*…so **DON'T LET IT AFFECT YOU**.

Just Say No!

There was an anti-drug campaign with the message and tag line "Just Say No", started by Nancy Reagan (President Reagan's wife) as part of the "War On Drugs". I'm not going into the politics of the "War on Drugs", but if you want to educate yourself on the negative effects of criminalizing drugs, it can make for some interesting reading and possible topics for you to write a school paper about.

What you *do* need to learn, however, is the power of saying no. People-pleasers are individuals who get into the habit of agreeing with whatever they are told. They don't want to seem disagreeable. They're afraid of upsetting other people. They want to make friends and just saying yes to everything is an easy way to avoid conflict. That **doesn't** make it right.

You need to develop the confidence and self-awareness to be able to say no when someone asks you to do something that you are against. Learning how to refuse something politely is a skill that you need to learn, yes, but don't be afraid to be clear and blunt when someone is trying to manipulate you into doing something that could hurt you.

Bullies

There are two types of bullies. I could divide them into more subtypes and explain the different psychological motivations that they have, but in the end, that level of research and classification is unnecessary: you don't need to know why someone is bullying you, you need them to **stop**!

First of all, you have the socially-motivated bully. Let's call this **Bully Type A**. He's the guy I talked about earlier. He puts you and others down because it makes him feel like he is socially superior to you. Because he thinks that by proving he is a bigger man than you, he'll get respect and attention, even the admiration of girls. And sometimes that is really how it works.

So how do you deal with these guys? To deal with *anything* in life, you need confidence. Once you have the confidence to confront your bully, the best way to deal with the situation is to expose what the bully is doing. Look at your bully seriously and ask him, "hey, bud, do you really think that making fun of me makes you a better person? If you put me down that makes you cool?"

The bully might have a response ready for you, something to try to shut you up. But whatever it is, keep pressing the point. Show them that putting you down does not mean anything. That it just shows how weak the bully is. The fact is that a **Type A** bully is just trying to assert his or her superiority, but as Eleanor Roosevelt said:

No one can make you feel inferior without your permission.

Don't give them that permission. If they want to bully you and insult you, let them know that it is sad and pathetic. That they are being *pathetic*. The only trouble with this is that it can go two ways. Either you are going to shut them up, or you are going to offend their little feelings. If they feel offended and are not able to shoot down your verbal arguments, a bully may use violence since he has nothing else left to do. You'll learn ways to deal with threats of violence in another section.

Bully Type B is another story, though. While regular people can be cruel and enjoy it, Type B is *sadistic*. This is the sort of person who enjoys hurting others and causing them pain. Where a Type A bully will do cruel things because he or she thinks that it gives them a leg-up on the social ladder, Type B bullies do cruel things because they *like* doing cruel things.

These are emotionally disturbed, immature people. There is no way to draw exactly where the limit is for these people. They may torture you every day that they see you, just because it gives them emotional satisfaction.

How do you deal with a Type B? In the same way that you deal with a Type A, **you have to be smart about how you interact with them**. Understand that when they are bothering you, they are getting enjoyment out of it. If you want to destroy the dynamic without things becoming physical ("avoid violence" is a good tenet to live by) you have to find a way to take the bully's pleasure out of the equation.

Example: let's look at **Jim.** Jim is a bully. He's big and he's chubby. When he goes home his parents treat him like crap. When he comes to school he treats *you* like crap. Mostly by making fun of you, but there is always the threat of him physically hurting you. And just to be realistic, Jim is NOT stupid. He's not an *idiot*, he just has emotional problems and family problems and he takes it out on you. What's the smart way to deal with Jim?

One approach you could take is to verbally confront him. Don't insult him. Don't try to make him feel stupid. The first tack you should take is to "befriend" him. Just open up and ask him why he is always picking on you. Tell him that you know he is not a stupid guy, that he has better things to do with his time, and that he would get more satisfaction out of having a friend than having a victim. If you have the verbal skills to suggest this to Jim the right way, you might be making a new friend instead of just dealing with a bully.

This is a simplistic scenario and obviously things will not work like this all the time. That's why your verbal and persuasive skills are important, so that you will be able to adjust your approach depending on your situation. Just as important is that you develop the other skills that will give you confidence and ways to deal with the bullies that you will encounter in life.

Your Bearing

Your bearing, the way you carry yourself, is where the psychological meets the physical. And it's very important. The next section of this book goes into improving yourself physically. This chapter, however, is to point out just how important it is that you carry yourself in the right way.

These are basic and general suggestions and while they are solid rules by which to carry yourself physically, taking them to the extreme may look ridiculous, so don't take it too far.

My uncle had a rooster called Jack. Jack didn't stick around for very long because he was a bully. But before he got his head knocked off, Jack used to run around puffing his chest out, blowing out his neck-feathers like a frilled lizard, and walking around like he owned the farm. Don't be like Jack. If he wasn't my uncle's rooster, I would have given him the boot every time he got close just because of the ridiculous way he puffed himself up, let alone the fact that he attacked me whenever I turned my back on him.

When you carry yourself, be confident, stand tall, and keep your shoulders squared. But don't look like a peacock or worse, an arrogant rooster. If you do, someone might come along and start making fun of you, and unless you have the confidence to take it well, you are just going to find yourself demoralized.

When you walk, walk with confidence. Keep your head level with the ground, keep your eyes at head level (you're allowed to look around, just don't be one of those sad people who keeps his eyes fixed on the ground). Have a little pep in your step.

How you conduct yourself with others also factors into this. If you are shaking someone's hand, shake it firmly, don't try to break their hand, but don't have a handshake that has no force behind it. When you are talking to someone, make eye contact and speak in a clear and normal (not too quiet) voice. Learn to radiate confidence and self-assurance in your body language. Non-verbal communication is very important and it is worth your time to practice yours and get feedback from people you trust who can be honest and objective with you.

The Magic Link

If there are any "secrets" in this book, this is it. The magic link. I mean, that's what I'd like to call it. Psychologists figured it out (not me) and it's a useful way to control your mood.

What is this magic link? It's the connection between your emotions and your body. There is a *real* connection between the way our bodies move and the way we feel and think. Has anyone ever told you that? Well try it out yourself.

Acting "happy" makes you happy. If you are feeling sad, upset, or disappointed, try it out. Jump around, dance, wave your arms in the air, smile. Put on the physical signs of being happy, act them out, and you will find that your mind actually starts "thinking" happy as well.

This is another reason why having a confident bearing is important. Walking with confidence will make you feel confident. Walking hunched over like a little ugly gremlin will make you feel like an ugly gremlin.

Try using this "magic link" to cheer yourself up. Do it in front of a mirror and see how your bearing changes. The people around you will be more receptive to you when you look happy and approachable as opposed to being shrunken and withdrawn, so it's definitely something that you should try out!

More on Confidence

In case I haven't said it enough, confidence is one of the most important qualities when it comes to attracting people to you and making friends. It's also an essential part in *everything* that you do in life. The tips that I have given you here may be enough for most people to start improving on their confidence.

Continue reading the rest of this book for more insight into how you can gain confidence. But if you feel like you need more advice specifically on being confident, I suggest you take a look at another of my books, **SOLID:** *A Guide to Gain Confidence and Get Rid of Insecurity.* It deals with the subject in-depth and in the same no-nonsense style that I've written this book.

Chapter Two: Physical

Physicality: *Why Your Body Matters*

In the last chapter, I talked about psychology. Understanding how people think gives you an edge in dealing with them and understanding their actions. Knowledge is power, and in the harsh world of high school, knowledge of the psyche is something that you cannot flourish without. Again, I'm not talking about *academic* knowledge here, although, the habits that I discuss later in the book provide a good framework in which you can balance school and life, this is social knowledge that we are discussing.

So yes, the mind is important. It's why I've devoted a whole section to it. Just as important as the mind, however, is the body. In many situations, physical superiority is more important than mental superiority, no matter how many times someone might have told you that *"the pen is mightier than the sword"*. They're usually talking about a pen that is being held by a guy who has plenty of metaphorical swordsmen at his command.

Why does your body matter? It's the first thing that people see. When people see you, strangers or friends, they are looking at your body, not at your mind. Until you can develop a reputation or wealth (usually later in life), people will look at you and see your physical state first and foremost. Yes, that is why your **Bearing** is important, as I talked about earlier. It's also why **Hygiene** and **Appearance** are critical, as I will talk about in a later section. But before all that, you need to look at your physical foundation: your body. Your physique. If it isn't what you want it to be yet, then think of it as a slab of marble. You can carve a masterpiece out of it if you want to.

Some of you might be surprised to read the following quote by the Greek philosopher Socrates, a guy who is one of the earliest and greatest thinkers in recorded history:

"No man has the right to be an amateur in the matter of physical training. It is a shame for a man to grow old without seeing the beauty and strength of which his body is capable."

Yes. That's one of the brainiest guys in history telling you that you should be an expert when it comes to physical fitness. He doesn't want you to grow old without ever unlocking your physical potential. So take it from him and make the decision to take care of your body because it's going to be the *only one you get.*

Being unfit usually comes down to one of two conditions: you are too **skinny** or you are too **fat.** Both of those situations are bad, and both of them can and will be addressed in this chapter. Of course, not everyone is one or the other. Maybe you're just average. In that case, you will need to incorporate some of what I say about both conditions to get the physique that you desire. What are the worst case scenarios? Well if you are **obese**, that is, excessively overweight, you are going to need to put in some more effort to get where you need to be, but you can do it and you had **better** do it! What about being **skinny-fat**, where your weight is "acceptable" for your height, but your muscle definition is too low and you are carrying fat? You look okay when you're in clothes, but when your shirt is off it's obvious that you aren't fit. Well, the solution is going to be the same for that as well.

Other than those two conditions, there may be one more problem. You may be physically incapable, for one reason or another, of achieving your body goals. You might be handicapped or limited in some way or another. In this case, you should do your best with whatever you have. That's all anyone can ask of you. If you have a condition that doesn't allow you to exercise much, it is okay. If you aren't the right height or your shoulders aren't broad enough, don't worry about it. Just improve in whatever way that you can!

Now, before we get into the nitty-gritty of fat loss and weightlifting, I do need to warn you about going off the other end. *Yes*, it's not great to look bad and be unhealthy. It's also not that great to **FEEL** bad and unhealthy. There's something called general **Body Dysmorphia**, a mental health problem where a person sees themselves as looking different than they actually are. Like a guy with massive muscular biceps seeing himself as skinny! Or a girl with a normal physique who thinks that she needs to lose a lot of weight. Do not let yourself get so obsessed with your body and what you see in the mirror that it has a negative effect on your life.

It's important to accept yourself the way you are and work towards improving to a better, stronger, healthier version of yourself. It's might be a hard balance to strike, but you should not hate your body or yourself.

Maybe you don't like it, sure, but take a positive and forgiving approach to self-improvement. As long as you are working to improve, you should cut yourself some slack.

Testosterone

As a growing male, most likely going through puberty, you have an edge that no one (probably) has taught you how to take advantage of. **Testosterone**. What is testosterone? Well it's only the most amazing chemical in the universe. Testosterone is the male hormone - secreted by your pituitary gland (in your skull) and later by your testes (your balls, son). What does it do? Oh boy.

Testosterone is responsible for all the stuff that happens to you in puberty. Your voice deepening. The growth of body hair. The growth of your penis and testicles. All that run of the mill stuff. But it also acts as the most potent muscle-building booster that you can naturally experience. What does this mean? It means that you have the chance, the opportunity, to build muscles while your body produces the sort of stuff that bodybuilders would like to inject to speed up their muscle development. Don't waste the opportunity.

If you want to take full advantage of this hormone bump, follow the advice in the next few chapters. Testosterone burns fat, builds muscle, and turns you into a hairy gorilla (to a degree). You may experience mood swings, or you might not. Just try to keep cool and focus on using this time to the best of your advantage.

Some things are known to help with testosterone production, like getting enough deep sleep, making sure there are enough fats in your diet (but not too much), having low stress levels, and exercising.

Fat Loss

The most important part of weight loss is dedication. Consistence and persistence are key to weight loss. It will take a long time maintaining the right habits for you to effectively lose weight. Sometimes you might slip up, it happens from time to time, but as long as you are persistent you will succeed.

Where do you start? Let's look at the building blocks.

What is fat?

It's an excess of energy stored in the form of fat cells that your body taps into when it needs it. I won't get into the chemical processes of fat-burning because I'm not a biologist, but it's important to understand the main principle of fat loss: CICO. Calories-In-Calories-Out. The calories that you take in must be less than calories that you burn (calories out).

You probably know what calories are, but let's define them anyway. Calories are a unit of measurement for energy (just like inches and feet are units of measurement). Nutritional information is usually printed on all the packaged food that you purchase, and learning how to count your calories and keep track of your daily calorie consumption is important. You can find online information on calories quite easily just by typing in a food followed by "calories" in a search engine, and there are apps and websites that can help you track your calories.

One pound of fat contains approximately 3500 calories (the number is closer to 3550, but most people have gotten used to quoting the 3500 figure). Your daily caloric use as a growing male will be approximately 2000 calories. There are online calculators that can give you a more accurate guess of your caloric demands based on your height, weight, age, and activity level.

But what you need to remember is that if you can create a deficit (negative difference) of calories, you will lose weight. Most dietitians will recommend that you avoid a deficit that is greater than 500 calories a day. With that deficit, though, you should be losing about one pound per week. How can you go about creating a caloric deficit?

Firstly, you are trying to build a better body. The main method for that is going to be exercise. That is the "calories-out" part of the equation and it will help.

But the critical part of weight loss is the "calories in" part of the equation. You have to eat less and eat healthier. What does that entail? Let's get into it.

Nutrition

Water. Make sure that you are hydrated. Drink those eight cups of water a day that are recommended. Make sure you have all the water that you need. Drinking water can help you handle your hunger and eat less. Along with that, coffee and tea are also great when it comes to weight loss. All useful things when it comes to weight loss.

Vegetables. If you hate salads, I'm sorry to tell you that they are a great tool when it comes to weight loss. Vegetables are low-calorie, high-fiber, and full of water, so eating them to feel full is the best option when it comes to weight loss. They make great snacks for weight loss. It depends on your tastes, but if you don't want to go through the effort of making a salad, you need to find easy veggies to snack on: carrots, cucumbers, celery, bell peppers.

Fruits. These are sweeter and higher in calories than most veggies because of their sugar content, but as long as you are eating whole fruits, then you are eating enough fiber along with the other parts of the fruit, to feel full. An apple or two, for example, make a great snack that is low in calories and satisfying. Fun, nutritious, and tasty, these are a great substitute to junk food and sweets. Fruit *juice* on the other hand is not low-calorie. You can enjoy juice from time to time, but do not assume that it is a "healthier" choice than water. It's better to eat your fruits than to drink them.

Carbohydrates. Carbs are the food that make up the majority of most people's diets (anywhere from 50% of your daily calories and up) and while they are not necessarily bad for you, you should cut down on carbohydrates when you are on a diet.

These come in two general types: refined carbohydrates (the bad stuff) and whole carbohydrates (the better stuff). Refined carbs are carbohydrates that have been processed and have very little nutritional value. Think macaroni or cornflakes.

Whole grains, on the other hand, are healthier than refined carbs. Things like whole oats, barley, quinoa, and beans are all better types of carbohydrate to eat than things like plain rice, bread, and pasta, not to mention French fries or mashed potatoes.

Protein. The most important part of your diet. These are the building blocks of your muscles and an excellent way to feel full. What proteins you eat will depend, mostly, on your finances, since this can be the most expensive part of your diet.

- **Eggs** are likely the most affordable and accessible source of protein available to you. The white of the egg is where all the protein is. The yellow yolk contains fats. Eating whole eggs is a great way to start your day, but if you are looking to cut down on calories, eating less of the yolk is an option.

- **Cheeses** are high in protein and high in fat, making them generally healthy, but not something that you should eat in very high quantities. Cheese sticks, for example, are a healthy snack, but with anywhere from 80 to 130 calories per stick, the calories can add up fast.

- **Nuts**. Nuts are not always cheap but they are one of the best foods for someone who is trying to lose weight. Nuts have high protein and fat content (the healthy kind of fat) and take your body a while to digest. This makes them a great snack food, delicious and long-lasting. Just watch out, they are still calorically dense and you should be careful that you don't binge on these.

- **Meat** is king when it comes to protein (although the quality of protein varies significantly). I'll break down the types of meat and how you should view them:
  - **Fish** are a great source of protein and healthy fats (you may have heard about healthy omega-3 fats. These are found in fatty fish like salmon) and are, arguably, the best source of protein. You should not eat too much fish too often, as they may contain mercury and lead, substances that build up in your body and can harm you. This usually only happens at very high consumption rates of certain kinds of fish, so you don't need to worry about this too much.
  - **Beef** is a great source of protein. When it comes to whole cuts of beef (steak, pot roast, etc.) you do not have to worry too much. The amounts of fat that are present are acceptable and healthy as long as the meat is not fried. Ground beef, on the other hand, comes with varying levels of fat (usually a percentage). If you are trying a strict diet, leaner percentages are better, but they're also more expensive.
  - **Chicken** is affordable and mostly healthy. At least, when it is baked, or cooked without too much oil. Fried chicken is *not* healthy. The "dark meat" of the chicken (the thighs and wings) is juicier and fattier, but not in a significant way, so if you prefer dark meat do not feel too bad about eating it instead of the breast, which is lower in fat and as a result much drier. It makes for better sandwiches or as a salad topping.
  -

- **Pork.** Bacon, oh that marvel of the Western world. Bacon is mostly fat and mostly unhealthy, but a few strips for breakfast will not hurt every so often as long as you try to eat more vegetables and less calorie-rich foods for another meal of the day. It *is* all about balancing your total calories. Less-fatty cuts of pork are somewhere between chicken and beef in terms of protein-to-fat ratios and are also an acceptable source of protein, just remember, portions do matter!

Fat. Fat is a component of a lot of foods. By weight, fat has about twice as many calories as protein or carbohydrates. It is not all bad, though. Your body needs fats to synthesize hormones and cell membranes, and your brain and nervous system also contain fats.

Don't try to cut out fats entirely, your body will suffer if you do.

What you *should* do, however, is cut down on sources of unhealthy fat. If you haven't already guessed it, this mostly has to do with (delicious) crispy, fried food. French fries, chicken strips, fried mac and cheese (what a terrible idea), most fried foods should be avoided like the plague if you are trying to lose weight. Actually, they should just be avoided in general.

The fat that you find from natural sources, like the fat in eggs, meat, fish, and chicken is not as bad as most frying oil fat.

Sugar. Foods that are primarily sugar-based, like desserts, should be eaten only on occasion and in small amounts. You should not drink sugary sodas at all when you are trying to lose weight. At 150 calories per can, one can of cola may be around a tenth of your daily caloric consumption. Diet sodas are better since they have almost no calories, but there are some questions about how healthy the aspartame sweetener is, along with the same negative effects of other ingredients like phosphoric acid.

Junk Food. Cut it out. That is almost everything that needs to be said about French fries, fast-food hamburgers (burgers made at home can be healthier), chicken nuggets, potato chips, hotdogs, you name it. They're all foods that are best avoided. Fast food should be an occasional treat, maybe eaten once a week, not a regular part of your diet.

The Mental Game

Now that you know what foods to eat and what foods to avoid, it's important to develop an idea of how to go about implementing your new, healthful diet.

Eat regular meals. Try to be as regular as possible with meal times and healthy snacks so that you do not find yourself getting too hungry. Having a routine when it comes to eating can help you with controlling what you eat. Find low-calorie snacks that you like to eat in between meals.

Befriend your hunger. This isn't advice to accept hunger and starve yourself, no. But if you are overweight or obese, chances are that you are not used to being hungry. Maybe you're the sort of person who reaches for some food just as soon as your stomach starts to rumble. Worse, you might have developed eating habits that involve munching on snacks when you aren't even hungry!

If you find yourself in such a situation, I suggest that you take some time learning to feel hungry again. Let your stomach rumble for an hour or two while you only drink water. Hunger is a signal from your stomach that it's time to eat, but an unhealthy diet and eating pattern may mean that your body has an unhealthy hunger signal. Relearn how to be hungry and find your willpower. It will help a lot to develop these natural cues now that you are learning how to eat healthy.

Portion control. The main thing to remember, when it comes to learning or relearning how to eat healthy is that portion sizes matter. If you go to a restaurant, sit-in or fast food, you are going to be over-served any way you look at it. A Big Mac has 560 calories in it. Throw in 350 calories for fries and you are already at 910 calories for a meal…assuming you drink water or a diet soda. That is already half of your daily calories. Now, granted, this has more to do with fast food being high in fat and calories, but the point is that restaurants do not give you food in healthy amounts. Go to a dine-in restaurant and take a look at the plate they give you. Chances are that the portions are much more than anyone should be eating in a single meal.

If you have gotten used to those portions, you are probably used to eating large amounts of food at home. This is a habit that you need to break. If you need to wean yourself off it slowly, try replacing the bulk of your meal with a salad, followed by the main dish, so that most of the fullness is from low-calorie veggies but you still get the satisfaction of eating "real food".

Emotional Eating. One of the most common causes of obesity is emotional eating. That is, when someone consciously or unconsciously eats and drinks food to feel better. This is an unhealthy eating behavior that might be a symptom of emotional problems, stress, or other problems in your life. If you notice that you eat a lot (binge) when you are upset or lonely, speak to someone who can help you, or look for other resources. I would recommend that you find positive activities that cheer you up, but sometimes the problem goes deeper than that, so talk to someone who knows your situation and is able to give you some insightful advice on how to deal with your problem.

Walking (and Running): *The Holy Grail of Physical Fitness*

When it comes to weight loss, walking is my favorite activity. Not because it's effective in itself, but because it's easy (unless you are very obese) and it gives you time to think. It's also proven that walking is good for your brain, mental health, and mood.

Walking for weight loss has to be part of a healthy eating regimen. If you walk for twenty minutes at a comfortable pace of 3 miles an hour, that's one mile. That burns around 100 calories. Walking for one hour will burn about 300 calories. If you have a head for calculations, then you can calculate that it takes about twelve and a half hours of walking to burn one pound. That's not very effective right? Well it depends on how you look at it.

Walk every day of the year for one hour and you would have burned an extra 90,000 calories. That's 29 pounds in a year with an easy, low-impact activity that allows you to do other things. My favorite thing to do while walking? Listen to podcasts. Listening to your favorite music is fine too, but an hour is a long time and it's more fun to learn new things or listen to news that you find interesting.

If you can find a walking-buddy, someone who you actually enjoy walking with, that's another great option. Otherwise, you don't even have to do anything but walk briskly and enjoy your surroundings. It will give you time to think as well, which is usually good.

Jogging is a faster way to burn calories. You can jog twice as fast as you walk, thus burning about twice as much calories per time spent running, *or* cutting your time in half to burn the same number of calories. But as a professor of mine once said: have you ever seen a happy jogger? Unless you actually enjoy jogging, your time may be better spent doing an exercise that you like more.

Running is the standard when it comes to building a solid base for your cardiovascular fitness. If you are in good enough shape, do it. Some people love it and others hate it. If you find that you enjoy running, it is something nice to be passionate about. It gets you in great shape, will have a positive effect on your mood (most exercise does this), and all it costs you is a good pair of running shoes.

Muscles

Don't pay attention to the people who tell you that lifting weights will make you shorter. That isn't how it works, it's just old science that hasn't caught up with the times. What *can* happen is that breaking or damaging the parts of your bones (epiphyseal plates) that are responsible for bone growth can result in your growth being affected. But regular sports and training will not do that, and as long as you are careful not to break your bones- it's really not that hard, I've never broken a bone in my life, at least up to the point of writing this- you shouldn't worry at all about lifting weights making you shorter.

What you *should* be careful about when it comes to lifting weights is proper form (you can find many free resources online for this) and not lifting too weights that are too heavy (when you are working with weights you can barely lift, you are much more likely to injure yourself). If you can lift weights in a safe setting with some adult/professional supervision, you will be just fine.

In any case, lifting weights is not the only way to get in shape. I already went over the great health benefits of walking in the previous section. I'm not huge fan of running, but as long as you have the right shoes and proper terrain, along with good running practices, you should be just fine.

Running develops your lower body quite well. Short **sprints** after warming up are preferable to steady-state jogging. Sprinting trains your muscles for high energy output in a short time. Jogging will maintain a high heart rate, and is good for fat-burning if you can handle the boredom, but it won't develop your leg muscles in the same way as sprinting while also placing wear and tear on your joints over time. If you are a real junkie for running and jogging, you can mix up your routine, alternating between the two (and incorporate walking) to come up with a nice mix, but as with all things, make sure that you get enough rest and don't push through injuries.

Sports, competitive or otherwise, are a great way to develop functional lean muscle.

- Basketball: high intensity, good mix of aerobic and anaerobic activity, develops hand-eye co-ordination. Watch out for knee injuries, this is one of the worst sports for it because of the rapid turns, twists and jumps.
- Football: High intensity, mostly anaerobic, lots of running,

shoving, and collisions. You can get hurt playing football worse than many other sports and the chance of sustaining concussions is very high. But if you like it, do it. As an amateur player, though, do not get yourself into too much trouble. It's not worth the long-term damage.

- Soccer: the perfect sport to stay lean and avoid the most damaging injuries. You'll spend most of your time running, so besides making sure to keep your knees from getting twisted, there isn't much to worry about. Just avoid cracking your shins against other people's legs and don't give yourself brain damage with too many headers.
- Other than those "Big 3" (you may want to add baseball, America's Favorite Pastime, or ice hockey) most other sports that you participate in for fun are great, just make sure to always take precautions to avoid injuries and don't get too competitive unless you plan on getting a scholarship or making a professional career out of it. As I said, it's just not worth the risk unless there is a real payout.

Martial Arts training is something that I can't recommend enough. There are many elements to self-defense that I will address in its own section, but being able to physically defend yourself is a crucial skill. The problem is that not all martial arts are made the same, and worse than that, the quality of training varies significantly from one school to another. There are any number of variations of martial arts styles and schools, and once you figure out which ones are available to you to learn, you should seek out the best affordable school that is near you.

In any case, learning how to defend yourself is an important part of being confident, so this should be a priority. Just avoid taking too many punches to your face and head in the learning process - you may end up with learning difficulties or a broken nose.

Pumping Iron

Weightlifting and bodybuilding are not the same thing. **Weightlifting** is a physical activity of moving heavy objects in some way or another so that you become stronger and better at lifting weights. **Bodybuilding** is a competitive sport where people use exercise, nutrition, and other supplements to grow their muscles to large sizes, shred off as much fat as possible, and then dehydrate and spray tan themselves before standing on a stage with other competitors and flexing in front of a crowd and judges. The terms are sometimes used interchangeably, but they are not the same thing even though the line of distinction can get blurry sometimes.

Now, this next part is more an opinion than a hard fact but I'll tell you anyway. Bodybuilding is not something that men do to attract women. People who want to attract others usually end up stopping short of the need to compete and become massive.

Bodybuilding is something that men and women do to soothe their egos. People with a desire to be huge, with a fear of being small, push their bodies to the limit so that they can look in the mirror and feel **awesome**. Does that make it wrong? Well, there are better things you can do with your life. But if you really want to dedicate yourself to getting huge because it will make you feel special, then who am I to stop you?

Most of us don't need to worry about bodybuilding. Chances are that it isn't for you. What *is* for you, or at least should be, is weightlifting.

Learn the muscle groups (Arms, Shoulders, Chest, Back, Core, Glutes, Legs) and muscles that comprise them. Then learn the types of exercises to target them. I'll make it a little simple for you. These are the general types of exercises for each muscle group.

- Arms: Biceps curls, Triceps pulldowns
- Shoulders: overheard press
- Chest: push-ups, bench-press
- Back: pull-ups, lat pull-downs
- Core: sit-ups, crunches, planks
- Glutes: squat, deep stairs
- Legs: squats, leg-press, stairs

Weight-lifters break up their exercises based on **Weight** lifted, number of **Sets** (a set is comprised of reps) number of **Reps** (repetitions of the exercise). Of course, you take a rest in between sets to let your muscles get their strength back. Anywhere from one minute to five minutes is normal.

For example, you might curl 20-pound dumbbells for 3 sets of 15 reps each. If you wanted to stimulate muscle growth you might increase the weight, number of sets, or number of reps, with different results based on which one you chose to increase.

As a general rule, lifting heavier weights will result in stronger muscles. Increasing the number of sets will improve your muscular endurance, and doing more reps will also boost endurance and muscular capacity.

If you do not want to lift weights, that is fine. There are still exercises that you can do at home, though you have to be careful that you aren't doing these on fixtures that can fall out or be damaged. The "no-gym exercise routine" simply consists of these few exercises.

Push-ups - these will target your **chest**, **triceps**, and shoulders

Pull-ups - pull yourself up while hanging from a horizontal bar, palms facing away: these will target your **back**, **triceps**, forearms, and shoulders

Chin-ups – pull yourself up while hanging from a horizontal bar, palms facing you: these will target your **back**, **biceps**, forearms, and shoulders

Planks - Get into a push-up position, but lean on your elbows instead of your hands. Hold this position straight and time yourself. This works your abs and other muscles in your core. 2 to 3 minutes in a plank positon is great.

Sit-ups/Crunches - sit-ups involve you lifting your whole upper body (from the hips up) and target your core. Crunches involve you curling the upper part of your torso off the ground and target the abs specifically.

Leg lifts - lying flat on your back, you can lift one or both legs, from your hips. Leg lifts will target your abs and core.

Squats - look up how to do these properly. They target your legs and glutes.

Stairs - walk or run up and down stairs outside. This will work your **thighs**, calves, and **glutes**.

Running - running improves your legs in general, but is also a good challenge to your cardiovascular fitness.

The Myth of "Spot Reduction"

Working a certain muscle group (your abs, for example) will not specifically burn fat from that area. What I mean is that you cannot get rid of belly fat by doing a lot of crunches. You can't get rid of a big butt by doing squats. When your body stores fat, it does so according to your physical make-up. When it burns fat, it will burn it from all over your body, regardless of what exercises you are doing.

Note to beginners: If you are a beginner weightlifter you will probably experience rapid muscle growth in your first few months if you are dedicated. Don't assume that this will continue once your body has "caught up" to what is normal.

Note: stretch marks are a normal part of building muscle. Do *not* buy expensive creams that promise to prevent stretch-marks unless they are recommended to you by a real doctor. Different people develop different amounts of stretch-marks. Your best option is to make sure that you are always well-hydrated, eating healthy, and rub skin creams (shea butter and cocoa butter are both good) that contain Vitamin E into your arms, chest, and other places where you are prone to gets stretch marks. But in the end, don't worry about stretch marks, worry about being fit, healthy, and strong!

Self-Defense

Before I get into the details of self-defense and the martial arts, I have to give you fair warning. Self-defense training should not be taken lightly. First of all, you are learning self-*defense*. What that means is that you aren't going out to learn how to beat people up. You are not learning how to fight (*okay, but you are, but that's not the focus*). You are learning new ways to protect yourself. This is a skill that you should only ever use if your physical safety or the physical safety of someone else is being seriously threatened. Many schools have zero-tolerance policies, and whether you were right or wrong to use force (even to defend yourself) you may find yourself suspended, expelled, or even facing criminal charges.

Does that sound excessive? Not really. Maybe a punch, a kick, or a shove will not grievously hurt the person that you do it to. But what if your strike knocks him off balance? And he falls backwards on to the sidewalk, cracks his skull, and ends up in a coma? What if he dies? Always remember that things like this can and *do* happen, and that using violence should only ever be a last resort.

When dealing with your safety being threatened there are usually several options. Some good and some not so good depending on the situation. The ideal approach is to de-escalate the situation verbally. If a bully is making advances towards you, use your words to reason with them. Try to get the attention of people around you for support. If that fails, another option is to get yourself out of that situation. There is no shame in running from a fight (as long as you aren't the one who started it. It's pretty bad if you go around starting fights and then run away).

EVEN IF SOMEONE IS PHYSICALLY ASSAULTING YOU, IF RUNNING IS AN OPTION, THAT <u>MAY</u> BE BETTER THAN FIGHTING BACK AND SERIOUSLY HURTING HIM OR GETTING HURT YOURSELF.

The second thing I have to warn you about is regarding your own physical wellbeing. Not all martial arts schools have your best interests at heart. In a boxing gym, for example, once a boxer has had enough training, sparring (controlled fighting) is naturally the next step. What you need to know, however, is that every punch to your head, whether it is by a gloved hand or not, has an impact on your brain. These can add up over a long time and leave you with the same "punch-drunk" effect as someone who has sustained serious concussions. Scientists still don't understand the full extent of damage caused by blunt trauma to the head, and they don't know how to prevent it either, for that matter. Another thing is that some trainers are not completely ethical in dealing with newcomers. If your new coach throws you into a fight soon after you start at his gym, that is not a good thing. A good coach will wait until you can defend yourself properly before he puts you into a serious fight.

The third warning is a general one, also regarding your health. It is possible that you go through your life never needing to learn how to defend yourself. Maybe it's not likely, but even in a situation where someone stops you and takes your wallet, you may not be in physical danger. Training in martial arts, *just* training, may mean that you get injured. You may damage your hands, wrists, arms, shoulders, and knees. So, by choosing to train in martial arts, you are putting yourself at risk of injury.

Is it worth it? If you are careful and take sensible precautions, you will eventually be better able to defend yourself and increase your confidence. You may find that you love training. It's an excellent way to deal with the stresses of life and keep yourself in good shape. I just need to warn you that it is not pain-free and it is also not risk-free.

Having said that, let's go over the martial arts that may be available for you to learn.

- **Karate, Tae Kwon Do, etc.** There are many Eastern martial arts, and they suffer from having too many different types and styles. On top of that, there are many schools that do not teach you real self-defense. Avoid schools that are "McDojos": places where you show up, are taught a few things to make you think you are a bad-ass Kung-Fu practitioner when, in reality, you have not learned how to defend yourself at all and are now just a few hundred bucks poorer having paid for a costume and belt. When picking a Karate/Tae Kwon Do school, make sure that you are going to learn from a sensei who is *really* going to teach you how to defend yourself.

- **Wrestling**, assuming that you have a wrestling program at your school, is a very useful sport to learn. While you will need to learn some method of effective striking (karate, boxing, etc.), learning to grapple and wrestle in close quarters is a great self-defense tool and the grappling training will give you strength and confidence. Wrestling is an integral part of some mixed martial arts styles.

- **Boxing** is my personal recommendation for learning how to defend yourself. All boxing comes down to is learning how to throw punches the right way while moving and leveraging your body effectively. In some ways, it's the most basic martial art, and it can be just as effective as any other. Boxing training is rigorous. After going for 3 minutes of high intensity sparring against a guy who is trying to knock your head off, you will start to get an idea of just how hard it is for championship boxers to go twelve rounds, not to mention the older fighters who had to go 15 rounds or, the original Marquess of Queensberry rules, where a fight would go on until only one man was standing. This is a tough and brutal sport, and while I enjoy watching it on TV or live, sometimes I wonder if it has any place in civilized society. But let's not worry about what grown men to do for a living or for their passion, find the nearest boxing gym and see if you can learn a thing or two.

- **Mixed Martial Arts, Muay Thai,** and **Kickboxing** to a lesser extent, are martial arts schools that are interdisciplinary. With the rise in popularity of MMA and the UFC, mixed martial arts have entered the public conscience and you are just as likely to find a gym that teaches MMA as to find gyms or dojos that teach the older martial arts. MMA training involves wrestling, grappling, and striking. MMA is a great option for learning self-defense, but you need to be careful. With all the different skills, there are many ways that you can get yourself hurt.

You need to read up on the different martial arts, research what your available options are, and watch videos of them being practiced so that you can make your own decision about what self-defense you want to practice.

One final piece of advice: I do *not* recommend general self-defense courses <u>at all</u>. These are usually geared towards women to teach them how to "handle" assailants, but self-defense is a physical skill and like all physical skills, it requires practice and repetition. A 5-week training course that teaches you 30 different techniques will usually result in you being unable to do a single one of those techniques effectively. As the late, great Bruce Lee said: *I fear not the man who has practiced 10,000 kicks once, but I fear the man who has practiced one kick 10,000 times.*

Practice one type of *real* self-defense for a few weeks and months to become competent and confident in your abilities.

Chapter Three: Social

Friendship

You need to make friends. I mean, that's the whole point of life for many of us. Humans are social creatures and most of us place social interaction and relationships high on our priorities list. The trouble is that some friends add to your life while others just take away from it. How do you choose? Well, let's lay out the basics first.

Be respectful, kind, and courteous to everyone. Unless someone gives you a reason to act negatively towards them, do *not* act negatively. If your gang of friends are making fun of someone, that doesn't mean that you have to pick their side and start harassing the person that they are harassing. This is a mistake that is easy to make either because you are trying to fit in and please others, or maybe you just think that your friends are right so you should support them. Don't. Unless you know the full context of a situation, **stay neutral!**

That aside, as I said, be respectful to everyone. And acknowledge that while you might like to be friends with someone, that person might not want to even look at your face. That's fine, move on, there are plenty of great people out there to hang out with.

What do you want to look for in a friend? You are looking for someone that shares the same values and interests as you. Someone who is intelligent enough for you to get along with (there are many kinds of smarts, but only one kind of dumb). Someone who has the moral character to not stab you in the back. It's not really a tall order is it?

Fine, if that is too optimistic for you let's go with what sort of people **not** to befriend:

- People with no redeeming qualities. If someone is lazy, rude and smelly, you probably don't want to be around them.
- Manipulative people. These folks are only out there to use others. You can still associate with them, but don't *trust* them.
- Drug abusers. I'm not sure how bad high schools are these days, but using illegal drugs is something you should avoid, and you should avoid being too close to people who are known to abuse them. More on this in a later section.

Other than that, just make friends with everyone. Don't limit yourself and don't box yourself into a specific group or clique. The music that you listen to should not define you (unless you're actually a paid musician, maybe). Your interests also should not limit the type of people that you make friends with.

Small Talk

One of those things that awkward people place too much importance on (whether teens or adult), there is nothing particularly complicated or difficult about small talk. All you need to do is pay attention to the person you are talking to (looking for cues that they are interested, uninterested, or annoyed) and a basic idea of what subjects are appropriate for small talk.

For your peers, movies, TV shows, sports, and classes are all general topics that you can shoot the breeze about. But once you know a person and some of their interests (do not stalk people online and talk to them about lasagna just because they posted about it, that will come off as creepy!) you can talk with them about anything. What's really important is to…

LISTEN.

If someone engages with you in small talk, or responds to you with eagerness, allow them to continue and pay attention to what they are saying. They are actually interested in telling you something! People will really appreciate it when you pay attention to them. This will make it much easier to be friends with them (although you don't need to force yourself to listen to someone talk non-stop just because you want to befriend them).

Note: do not spend a lot of time listening to girls under the assumption that this will make you friends and *then* you might have a chance to ask her out. No, there is a huge difference between being a friend and being a boyfriend. If you want to ask a girl out, you need to ask her out after you get to know her just a little bit and if she seems interested. Do NOT befriend her *just* because you are too chicken to ask her out. Befriend her because you want to be friends with her.

Athletics: *Scholarships, Belonging, and Achievement*

I wasn't an athlete in high school or college, so I haven't personally experienced the rigors that it takes to commit yourself to a sport. But I made friends with many who were, so I can give you an observer's opinion, and since it's objective, it's worth a lot more than having an athlete talk about it, especially since jocks are stupid. Just kidding, that is actually a huge stereotype and it's best that you drop it completely.

Athletes are more likely to be motivated and driven than your average gamer or couch potato. They are more active and, on average, just as intelligent if not more intelligent. Yes, that really sucks doesn't it? That you can't look at someone who is taller, stronger, and fitter than you and say "well, maybe he's *physically* superior, but he hasn't got my brains." Well, you're going to have to get over it, because you need to get busy improving yourself.

Now, not everyone is cut out for sports. If you are shorter than six feet tall, you haven't got much of a chance at being a competitive basketball player. Even *at* 6'0, you need abnormal skills, speed, and co-ordination to make the team. Similarly, you will not be very competitive in American Football if you are not larger than the average guy, and stronger as well.

Some sports are more forgiving when it comes to physical dimensions. Soccer for one, is played equally well by average-size people. Baseball relies more on natural gifts like hand-eye co-ordination and reflexes. Swimming is another sport that might work for you without you being naturally bigger.

But all of these sports and activities take commitment and dedication for you to excel in. Besides the possibilities of injury (I know, it's a theme that has come up a lot when discussing things, but you only get **one** body and you don't want to start crippling it before you even hit the half-way point of life) participating and excelling in sports is something that I can't recommend enough to you. There are three main reasons why you should get into any sport that you can while in high school.

The first reason is **scholarships**. Depending on your sport and how good you are in it, you will find that many colleges offer scholarships to their athletes. In some cases, a full-ride scholarship. In others, less. But if you're very good in a sport, being sought out by the coaches, you may be able to get into a college that otherwise would not have even considered you simply based on your academic merits.

The second reason, and just as important, is the feeling of **belonging.**

Most people have a need to belong. To be able to identify as something. Using a sport to define yourself is a shortcut. Maybe not the best one, but, at least it is something. Being part of a sports team or program will give you a sense of belonging and camaraderie with your teammates. While it is somewhat artificial (you aren't going to like everyone on the team), it also gives you the chance to make lifelong friendships with the people that you are surrounded by.

The last reason is because athletics give you the opportunity to have a sense of **achievement**. You will be able to look on your performances, games, meets, as achievements. Something to be proud of. This can have a huge impact on building your confidence and sense of identity. On top of this, *others* may ask you about those achievements. Being successful in a sport will make you look better to them, whether we are talking about college interviews, future employers, or new acquaintances.

This isn't to say that choosing to commit to an athletic program will be easy. In high school it will take up a chunk of your time and a lot of your energy. In college it only gets worse, with trainings sometimes scheduled in the early morning before any classes start at all. You will also be on the road a lot, missing some classes, in order to travel for competitions and meets. So it's not a decision to take lightly. But the commitment and dedication that you develop while participating in a sports program is character-building and will also instill you with discipline.

Do not limit yourself when it comes to choosing an athletic program. Even cheerleading is fine, as long as it's something that you find enjoyment in. The only issue is that you make sure that you balance the demands of your sport with the importance of being successful in your academics.

Hobbies

Be careful not to waste your time on your hobbies. Just because you like something it doesn't mean that you should spend a lot of time on it. Unless your hobbies can result in giving you skills or connections that are valuable to you, they are mostly a liability and an ineffective way to spend your time.

Gaming, playing video games, is a fun activity, but unless you seriously plan on being a game designer (not as fun as it sounds, and not as easy, for that matter) or to fly drones, there are better things to waste your time on. A little gaming may be fine, but spending too much time (more than a couple of hours a week) on a video game is a very stupid waste of your time. Practice your hand-eye coordination doing something better.

Playing **sports** as a hobby is great: you can stay in shape, make friends, and get the exercise that is an important part to regulating your mood. But balance this with the risks of injury. Football, soccer, and basketball among other sports, can result in you sustaining life-changing injuries. Just look at people who have torn ligaments in their knees and required surgery and long periods of rehabilitation. So unless you are playing sports to get into college, or maybe even to be a professional, it's a good idea to go easy on yourself and learn as much as you can about how to prevent injury and stay healthy.

Playing **musical instruments** isn't a bad hobby, but like most hobbies, it will take you a long time to get really good at it, and unless you are blessed with a great singing voice, you are going to have to find other people to play with if you want to get chicks with your music. Playing violin or piano, the classical stuff, is difficult to do well, requiring hours and hours of practice if you weren't born a savant. So unless you are a natural musician, don't waste a whole lot of time on this.

Art is kind of similar to music: it's difficult for the average person to be very good and unless you see yourself doing something that involves drawing skills, like architecture or design, you will be wasting your time. Do some art if it is important to you, but don't expect anything to come of it unless you are able to leverage your skills for a future job (graphic design is another one where this hobby would come in handy).

Writing is a great skill to develop, especially if you plan on getting into an academic career. **Reading** also falls into the same category. The more you read and write, the better your grasp of the language. This is a hobby that you should cultivate with a moderate amount of reading every day, along with putting in effort into developing your writing. Reading the news is a good basic exercise, and if you plan on getting into a finance career, reading the finance pages in the newspaper is a good way to begin learning about the markets and business in general.

Computer skills, like learning how to set-up a spreadsheet with functions, formulas, and graphs aren't exactly hobbies, but they are skills that are worth developing. Practicing with graphic design, or basic website design is also a useful computer hobby. **Gaming** on the computer is not.

Programming. This isn't even a hobby any more. Programming is an investment of your time. If you want to enjoy high school, learning programming may eat up a whole lot of your time. But learning how to program computers and applications is one of the most important skills in this new age and if you have a natural inclination towards it, go ahead and immerse yourself, you can't go wrong.

Other Hobbies: you can make a hobby out of anything. What I suggest is that you dedicate yourself to hobbies that fulfill two conditions. (1) Hobbies that you enjoy, and (2) hobbies that will help you be successful. If it doesn't fulfill both of these, it probably is not worth dedicating too much of your time to it.

Clothing

Chances are, you don't have much money to waste on clothes. Well, that's okay. What you will wear depends on your tastes, but there are a few simple rules that you need to remember, regardless of what your budget looks like.

1) Clothes cost money. Unless your parents are pretty well off, you shouldn't just go off and buy the latest brand-name clothes. I'm talking about the high-end stuff where you are paying 3 or 4 times as much for a polo shirt because it's got an alligator on the front. That alligator isn't going to make you faster, prettier, or smarter. Maybe *some* people are going to think that you're cool because you have enough money to waste on alligator-icon shirts. How about finding better ways to impress people?

Shakespeare said, *"the clothes make the man."* I'm not suggesting that you be shallow (everything in this book should be telling you the opposite) and preoccupy yourself with your appearance, but as we've already seen, the way that you look has a huge effect on the way other people see you and, even more importantly, the way you see yourself.

So you are going to need to figure out ways to get the right clothes at the right price for your budget. If this involves going to thrift stores or getting other types of used clothes, there's nothing wrong with that (just wash the clothes before you wear them). Ask around your neighborhood, or online. Look for garage sales. Whatever works. Just don't go shoplifting. It's not worth going to a juvenile court over clothes.

2) Reality number two is a tough one. Clothes can only look so good on an unattractive body. Why do fat people generally wear baggy clothes? Because they don't look attractive in tight form-fitting clothes. The problem with this is that baggy clothes do not compliment your figure either (**note**: to be fair, some people find fat *attractive*. To be realistic, most people do *not*).

There are two ways to address this issue. The first approach takes time, and you *will* be working on it. It's the approach of losing fat and building muscle. It may take you several months, but with persistence, you will lose weight, look better, and be able to wear better-fitting clothing.

The second way to address this issue is the one that you will go with in the meantime. As long as your pants or shorts are a good fit (and make sure they are a good fit, *no one needs to see your ass crack*) the main issue when it comes to clothing is your upper body. While following the guidelines of *fit* that I will talk about next, you would also benefit from wearing more than one layer of clothing (two is generally the most you can get away with if it isn't winter). What do I mean by that? If the temperature is cool enough, don't just wear a t-shirt or polo. A light jacket (denim or cloth) or shirt that is a good fit for you can complement your appearance. Not a vest, though. A vest will just make you look fat if you're fat. Go online and search for style ideas.

This isn't an attempt at hiding your weight (don't be self-conscious about it), you're wearing an extra layer to look good. This shows good taste in general, and is always a good thing to practice.

3) The third reality is that not all sizes across all brands are the same. Different shirts and pants will vary by cut, width and length even if they have the same size designation. What does this mean? Shop around and don't buy something unless you can tell that it's perfect for you! Suppose I'm shopping for a polo in a department store. The **medium** polo was too tight on my chest but just the right length. Their **large** size polo was a good fit for my chest, but it reached to half-way past my butt. They're both on sale for $12, so which one should I buy? NEITHER. The right thing to do is to find other brands that have better dimensions to suit your body.

If clothes don't fit you just right, don't waste your money on them. Sometimes, with body changes, a shirt that was too tight might fit better, or jeans that you couldn't fit into before become your regular day-wear. But in general, when you go out to spend money on clothes, do not waste your money on things that will not look good on you.

Note: the only exception to this is when you are looking at things like a clearance sale or garage sale where you would be paying a *fraction* of the normal price for clothing that you honestly expect to fit into in the near future.

So what do you need to learn from this? You need to learn how to dress the part of someone that is clean, smart, and self-aware. Unless you plan on having a career where looking frumpy is acceptable (mad scientist, hermit, castaway), you need to dress right, and the sooner you start paying attention, the better. Let's go over some fashion basics.

1. Wear clean clothes. Your clothes should always be clean and smell clean.

2. Iron your clothes. Other than jeans, most of your clothes will get wrinkly, so make sure they are ironed when they get too wrinkly.

3. Vary your wardrobe. Don't wear the same clothes over and over again. People will notice.

4. **Y**ou can break rule 3 when it comes to jeans. As long as they are clean and tidy, you can wear the same pair 3 times a week.

5. Tuck dress shirts in while wearing a belt. Never tuck a polo or t-shirt in.

6. Learn to roll up your long shirt sleeves properly (here, I'm talking about long-sleeve shirts). This may cause the sleeves to wear out, though, so only do this with a shirt that you prefer to wear with the sleeves rolled up. Keep a nice shirt or two that you do not do this with.

7. Learn the basics of formal wear, and take some time to practice dressing up in a shirt, tie, and suit. Yes, this means that you need to learn how to tie a tie. It's not as crucial while you're in high school, but the sooner you learn how to dress up, the better.

8. Buy good-quality belts. Some fabric belts, if they fit your style, are acceptable and durable. When it comes to synthetic leather belts, however, quality is hardly assured. Buying real leather is usually better and it doesn't have to be too expensive for casual wear (Aeropostale for example, have durable leather belts). Fancy formal belts are also affordable, just make sure that the hardware of the buckle is sturdy and not likely to fall apart (tip: reversible belts, while versatile, have buckles that are more likely to break).

Shoes

If you are really into fashion, shoes are going to be an expensive part of your wardrobe. You need to be smart about what and when you buy them. And you need to learn to take care of them. Shoes come in a few different types. I'm not an *expert* on shoes, so do some more research if you really want to get into the many details of different styles and materials.

Athletic shoes: if you participate in sports, whether for school or for fun, you are going to need some quality sports performance shoes. There are different types (running shoes, basketball, football and soccer cleats). Read up on heel and arch support if you have any foot problems and consult a podiatrist. Good athletic shoes are expensive but the right pair is worth it.

Sneakers: also called tennis shoes or trainers. These are also a type of athletic shoe, good for being active and also comfortable, but not necessarily high performance. Sneakers can be fashionable and comfortable.

Converse Chucks, Vans, etc.: Types of shoes that are more for fashion than they are for hard performance. Converse's Chuck Taylor series of shoes were worn by old-timey basketball players and then became a defining element of, *Nirvana* singer, Kurt Cobain's wardrobe. These types of shoes are fine for casual wear, coming in many different shapes and colors.

Formal and semi-formal shoes: There are many variants of dress shoes, and other semi-formal shoes. You probably only need a pair or two at most for formal functions. When it comes to dressing up formally, the only rule you will want to remember from here is that your belt and shoes should match.

Personal Hygiene

Personal hygiene isn't a complicated subject. Take a shower every day. With soap. Wash your hair. clean yourself thoroughly. Shave your pubic hair if it starts getting too long. Wear deodorant. Nobody wants to be friends with someone that looks or smells like they don't shower.

Okay, maybe I am simplifying it a bit too much. Let's go through them one by one.

Shower every day: this one isn't exactly fixed in stone…you could get away with showering 4, 5 or 6 times a week. But at your age, body odor is a thing…a really bad thing. So unless you happened to have a day where you stayed completely clean, then *maybe* you could go a day and a half without showering. Either way, it's better to just do this. With soap, obviously.

Clean yourself thoroughly: you are the only person who is cleaning yourself. That means you had better do a good job when it comes to your pubic area and your butt. Neglecting to keep your private parts clean will not go well for you. On the topic of your butt…did you know that toilet paper isn't really enough? Maybe if you were a lumberjack who spent most of his time in the woods, yeah. But in many places of the world, people wash with water after taking a dump. There is no reason why you shouldn't as well. Then dry off with toilet paper after you've washed clean.

Facial hair: you probably aren't going to have a lot of facial hair in high school. The best things for you would be to get a $20 electric trimmer to trim it off when it gets long. You can also use the trimmer on your armpits and pubes, but don't tell anyone because they won't like you if you tell them that you shave your mustache and pubes with the same trimmer.

Armpits: the home of sweaty, hormone-boosted body odor. Wash them with soap every time you shower. Apply deodorant every day. Some people are under the impression that shaving your armpits, as a man, means you're effeminate or gay. Don't pay attention to them. If you prefer to shave your armpits, that's just fine.

Pubic hair: if you maintain good washing practices this is not as critical, but it's a good idea to keep it from growing too long. Machine clippers are a much safer option than scissors, but they can both cut your skin and the last thing you want is to cut the skin of your pubic area. Shaving with a regular plastic razor is somewhat easier, and when done right, is not likely to result in you cutting yourself. It will take some practice.

Note: do not use someone else's electric clippers to shave your pubes. That's not okay.

Nails: get your own nail-clipper and practice taking good care of your fingernails, cutting them on a weekly basis. Also practice keeping your nails clean. It isn't nice to have dark dirt under your fingernails. Keeping your nails trimmed will help with this, as will washing your hands and taking regular showers.

Note: when it comes to clipping your big toes, be careful to do it right. Look up "ingrown toenails" and talk to an adult for advice on how to prevent them.

Cologne: real brand perfumes are expensive and they are not something that you *need* in high school, but if you can afford a bottle of high-end cologne, find a scent that you like, (preferably one that is not so strong that people will smell you before you've entered a room,) and spray it on your neck when you want to be a little fancy. Maybe keep it reserved for when you have special functions to attend, or a date to go on.

If you are trying to stay within a budget, a spray-on deodorant is fine, but do *not* apply it the same way that you would cologne. Spray it on your armpits as usual, and if you want a bit more, a quick spray on your chest (under your shirt) is the way to go. That way, no one is going to smell you until they are pressed up against you. You aren't trying to let the whole world know what deodorant you wear.

Socks: I don't need to tell you that you should **wear clean socks every day**. Unless you have magic feet or something, your socks are going to smell pretty bad if you don't change them. Then your shoes are gonna start stinking. So, just do what I tell you, and wear new socks every day. Some extra tips for you:

- Buy 10 or 15 pairs of the same color and style socks, then put them all in the same drawer. You won't have to worry about mismatched pairs and you can throw individual ones out as they wear out.
- Darker socks don't look as dirty. A pair of white socks can start looking permanently dirty after being worn a few times.
- Have a few pairs of dress socks for when you wear your dress shoes.

Drugs

Some people would advise you to get informed about drugs. "Don't just say no, but know what you are saying no to!" is their stance. Well, that's not a bad stance to take, but when it comes to high school, drugs, and peer pressure, "no" is usually the only right answer. In this section, I'm just going to go over the main things I think you should know.

Tobacco:

Cigarettes, cigars, chewing tobacco, and the newest trend, "e-cigarettes/vapes/e-hookahs". These are all products that contain tobacco, or the active ingredient in tobacco, nicotine. I've been a smoker for many years, but if you asked me, I think it would be great if tobacco was no longer sold. What's great is that data shows smoking to be on the decrease among young people.

It smells bad, tastes bad, and shortens your life expectancy. So why would anyone smoke? Because it's addictive. As Mark Twain said: *giving up smoking is the easiest thing in the world. I know because I've done it a thousand times.*

Nicotine gives you a feeling of satisfaction because it triggers the reward system of the brain. Every time you light up and inhale a cigarette your brain thinks "oh, this is great. This feels really good". At first you don't feel it, but over time, you become dependent on this feeling. If you spend too much time without it, you become uncomfortable and irritable. So you end up paying money to inhale burning stuff just to feel normal.

If you never smoke a cigarette or cigar, you'll be just fine. If you *do* want to be a smoker, wait until you're 18 before you commit to spending thousands of dollars on something that will make you smell bad and get sick.

As for the newer "vapor delivery" methods, the jury is still out on them. They may be safer than conventional smoking methods, but anything that contains nicotine is going to be addictive in the long run. Like I said, wait until you're eighteen.

Alcohol:
Alcohol *is* a drug, and it's one of the most destructive drugs that are allowed in society. I'm not exaggerating. Every year thousands of people are injured in drunk-driving accidents. Thousands and thousands more suffer from the long-term effects of alcohol abuse. I'm not even going to pull up the statistics. Go look them up yourself and see just how bad this drug is.

Alcohol is a drug that can be enjoyed in moderation once you are old enough, but research shows that it can affect brain development in people who haven't matured fully, so just like tobacco, I'm gonna suggest that you leave it until you are old enough.

Note: alcoholism seems to run in families. Part of this may be genetics, and part of it may be a learned behavior. In any case, avoid patterns of alcohol abuse, whether you are old enough to drink it or not.

Marijuana:
"Oh but what about the harmless drugs? No one ever died from marijuana!"

It's possible that no one has ever died directly from smoking marijuana. But plenty of people have been hurt, injured, or even killed while doing things while they were impaired. As if that isn't bad enough, plenty of people end up in jail with criminal records for possessing these "harmless" drugs because they live in places where it is a criminal offense to possess marijuana or be high on it. At your age, especially if you are in a state or country where it is illegal, you should stay as far away from these drugs as possible.

Note: you will have more than enough time to experiment in college, and as marijuana laws become looser over time, you can look forward to blazing up legally when you are older.

Hard Drugs:
I'm going to put everything else under this category. Some of these are illegal drugs while others are prescription drugs, still illegal to have without a doctor's prescription. You really shouldn't be touching any of these while you're in high school or ever. You are too young to be getting in trouble for drugs when there are plenty of other things you could be doing.

Relationships

I'm going to have to write a *whole other book* on this one. Seriously, the art of romance is complicated and a pain in the ass. Follow most of the advice in this book and you shouldn't have too many problems. If you like a girl your best chances are to be confident and cool (like I said, work on the stuff in this book and you will be fine). It's important not be seem desperate.

The best advice I can give you is to not give too much of a damn. You're young and you've got more than enough time to find the right person for you. Most of the relationships in high school don't go very far anyway.

Sex

This is a contentious subject. To get in depth, I'd have to talk about this in another book, along with "Relationships". Here I'll just leave the cliff notes of why you should wait until you're older (*and keep an eye out for my upcoming book on relationships and sex*).

The positives: It feels good.

The negatives: you can get sexually-transmitted diseases (STDs) from sex, some of which are permanent and some that are treatable. You can get a girl pregnant. This is so not worth it, especially at a young age when you cannot even support yourself, let alone someone else.

I could keep going on and on about the negatives but I don't want to give you a lecture. If you do decide to have sex, **educate yourself on all the ways that you can protect yourself from getting a disease and for preventing pregnancy**. Both of these fall under "safe sex". Do *NOT* have sex until you have learned <u>everything</u> there is to know about practicing safe sex.

Chapter Four: Odds and Ends

Acne

Acne is a problem that many teenagers have to suffer from. There are different kinds, from pimples all the way to the reddish inflammations that can leave those distinct facial scars. If you are experiencing serious acne, consult a dermatologist. There are several strong medications that can treat acne completely but they need to be prescribed by a professional.

Go online and read about other people's experiences. Don't apply any home remedies that may leave permanent scarring on your face. If you are going to pop your pimples, learn when and how you can do it properly. You don't want permanent scars on your face just because you wanted to pop a pimple.

Loose Skin

Loose skin is something that you may experience after drastic weight loss. Your skin (your body's largest organ) is elastic, especially when you are still in your teens. It may take a year or two before loose skin tightens up, but in the meantime do not let it affect your self-image too much. Adding muscles to your frame will help you look better, and if you end up having too much loose skin after weight loss and time has passed, you can consult a doctor about plastic surgery to have it removed.

Man Boobs

There are two kinds of "man boobs" on a guy. The first is just fat. When you are overweight, fat builds up on different parts of your body, and having fat on your chest may give you the appearance of having breasts. In this case, though, it's just fat, and it will go away with weight loss.

The other type has the scientific name, gynecomastia (also called "gyno" informally). This is the development of actual breast tissue in a man. This is not something to be ashamed about, as you are going through puberty, your hormones may put your body through a lot of different chemical changes. Puffy nipples may indicate that you are experiencing some degree of gynecomastia. If you are concerned that it may be abnormal, don't be afraid to talk about it with your parents and consult your family doctor.

Warning: don't talk about it with your friends. Really. You are probably going to get made fun of until your friends mature, which may take forever. A slang term for gynecomastia is "bitch tits" and I doubt you want that to become your nickname.

Body Hair

You probably won't have a whole lot of body hair in high school, but if you do start growing hair in unwelcome places, don't be ashamed of it. If you really want to, go ahead and find out how to get rid of it.

Penis Size

Oh boy, this one is a headache. As a growing teen you might have a lot of pressure on you to measure up to many standards. In this case, "measure up" is quite literal. You're still growing, though, so give yourself some time and don't obsess about the size of your junk. You still have time to grow.

If it is looking like a real issue, talk to a parent or doctor. You should not be ashamed of your body.

Family Problems

Family problems come in all types. I could write a whole book about everything I can think of and there still would be issues that I don't address. And I'm not a psychologist or counselor, so I doubt it would be a very good book.

What I can say here is that having a dysfunctional family is not unique, though each family has its own unique *problems*. Having divorced or unmarried parents, or alcoholic parents, or siblings that you don't get along with can all have huge negative impacts on your life. It's not really fair, but coming from a problematic home may make it harder to be successful in life.

Strong family relationships are important so, if you can, work hard to improve them. If you find yourself in the middle of a war between your estranged parents, look for advice on how to protect yourself emotionally. You aren't responsible for the troubles that other people put themselves in.

If you are having trouble with abusive parents, seek help. There are resources out there. Trusted friends are a great support system, so confide in them, but be ready to reach out to adults as well.

Don't be ashamed to seek help from a counselor or trusted friend when it comes to these things. Problems at home can set you back for life. The sooner you address them, the better.

Breakups

If you find yourself in a relationship and then find yourself *out* of one, don't get too depressed. Talk to an older person that you can confide in and be open about how you feel. Even if you are smart enough to know that young relationships are not meant to last, it can still be difficult to get over a breakup but talking about it helps.

Depression and other mental health problems

It's difficult to tackle serious problems on your own. If you feel that you have mental or emotional problems, find someone that you can trust. Speak to a parent, counselor, or trusted teacher. Ask for help. There are many tools that you can find to help you, but you have to have the courage to reach out and ask for help. If you are not comfortable opening up to the people around you, look online for information. But before you decide to "diagnose" your problem based on things you read, I strongly advise you to speak to a professional or at least an educated adult that you can trust.

Chapter Five: Vignettes

I've written a few general scenarios in this section that outline problems and the ways I suggest you deal with them. You may not fit into any of these categories, but you may experience some of these issues. Read through them and get a feeling as to how you should handle these common issues.

The pipsqueak

Jim is smaller than most of his classmates. He's skinny and short and is often the target of bullies and ridicule because of it. What would I tell Jim to do?

The first thing that Jim should do is understand what leads his bullies to harass him. Is it just because he is small? Or is there something in the way that he reacts (or doesn't react) that spurs them on and encourages them to continue?

Jim needs to start working out to put on muscle. I'd recommend that he also starts to practice self-defense of one kind or another. This isn't because he needs to physically attack his bullies, but getting stronger and more adept at self-protection will give Jim more confidence. He also should find other things that boost his confidence and give him the courage to verbally confront his bullies.

Jim needs to TELL them to STOP bullying him. There is nothing wrong with getting an adult involved in this situation if the bullying is too intense and Jim is afraid for his own safety. There's also nothing wrong with seeking friends to stand with him when he confronts the bullies, but do not expect them to fight for him. He also should not make a huge scene when there is no adult supervision because a bully will not like being challenged in front of a large group of students (he will want to send a message that he is the top dog and put Jim "back in his place").

With enough exercise and strength, Jimmy will no longer be a pipsqueak. Even if he remains shorter than the average classmate, he can still be strong and confident, and strong little guys can still pack a punch!

The geek

Ben is a geek. He has never been a fan of physical exercise, instead playing on his computer and videogames. He does great in school (or maybe he doesn't), but his extra-curricular activities involve sitting at a desk and playing an MMORPG. What should Ben do to improve his life?

Well, the first thing the "geek" needs to do is look at his hobbies and how they are impacting his life. Chances are (unless you are some kind of gaming champ) your MMORPG will never give you anything except a fake sense of progress. Those games are *designed* to be addictive. Ben needs to cut his gaming down drastically, to no more than 1 hour a day at most, and hopefully even less.

If Ben really loves sitting on the computer, he should "play" something that gives his life real value. He should learn some programming or graphic design. Maybe invest some time in learning to make a website. Or researching subjects that he is really passionate about. Even writing a blog will be superior to wasting your time on a video game.

The next thing that Ben should do is work on developing his social skills. Finding any physical sport to practice, whether at a club or with friends, is a great idea. If that isn't an option, for one reason or another, Ben should find friends in some other type of club or activity. Getting out and socializing face to face is something that every geek can benefit from.

The fat guy

Alex is fat. He's been fat for as long as he can remember. People like him (or maybe they don't) but nobody looks up to him, or admires him. Alex may make jokes about his weight, or maybe he doesn't. But he finds himself being the butt of many people's jokes. Even his friends call him fat, though they don't always mean it in a harsh way. What should Alex do?

Alex needs to read the basics of my advice on how to eat and exercise for weight loss. Weight loss is not a complicated thing, but it takes hard work, dedication, and **persistence**. If there is a sport that Alex can participate in, he should. Even if classmates will make fun of him. Alex just has to prepare himself and work on being mentally tough enough to take the criticism and negative things that are thrown at him and believe that he will continue to improve and work on losing weight.

Along with (or instead of) participating in sports, Alex needs to start exercising on his own and monitoring what he eats. Remember that weight loss does not happen all at once. Its's like chipping away at a marble block every day to carve out your statue. At first it doesn't look like anything at all. But after one month, and another, and another, huge changes will start to show. Alex should focus on building muscle along with burning fat.

The awkward and quiet guy

Joe doesn't know how to talk to people. He isn't exactly shy, he just doesn't know what to tell the guys, or even worse, the girls. It seems like he just isn't good at conversation. What should Joe do?

First of all, Joe needs to understand that he doesn't have to say *the perfect thing* every time. If he is worried about saying something stupid, that is fine, but too much importance is placed on small talk. Joe should read my section on small talk and see ways that he can improve.

Along with that, Joe should watch some stand-up comedy. No, don't steal comedians' jokes, that is stupid. But practice the easy way that they deliver their lines. Their confident body language. As I said before, a confident stance will make you *feel* more confident. So just square up your shoulders, stand tall, and relax. Loosen up, Joe.

The shy guy

Alan is shy. He's scared of talking to people. He's scared of what they think about him. So he just shrinks into his seat, and talks his one or two friends. What does Alan need to do?

Alan needs to understand that most people will not bite. Alan may be scared of **humiliation**. As social creatures, this is one of the things that many of us are wired to be most afraid of. The chances of him being dramatically humiliated are really small.

Alan needs to push himself to participate in class, join any clubs or activities that appeal to him, and interact with people. He needs to commit to eradicating his shyness. It's only hard at first. Once you realize that people don't bite, and aren't out there just waiting to pounce, Alan will realize that everyone is a human being and talking to them, wherever you find them, is just fine.

The End

This has been a whirlwind of opinions and advice and I think it's probably too much to take in all at once. But take it all one step at a time and practice implementing the advice and suggestions that I have made. Find ways to balance the mental, physical, and social aspects of your life while also balancing your school life and academic success.

Life is a balancing game, yes. But in the end, after everything is said and done and you've read and learned every little thing that is supposed to help you, it all comes down to one simple truth: be yourself. **BE YOURSELF.** Not in the lazy, "if you aren't good enough for them then they don't deserve you" way, no. That doesn't work very well unless you are already super amazing.

No, being yourself means knowing who you are and what you want. Not necessarily what you want to do, or where you want to go in life, but those are parts of it too. Being yourself means that you know what is important to you. That you live your life according to how you want to live and grow. That you develop healthy relationships with people that you value and that you learn to be happy by yourself as well.

Take all the advice I give you in this book and practice it to improve yourself. Keep learning and never stop growing. In the end, you're going to need to be happy with yourself and where you go in life, and blaming others will not make things better. So focus, *focus, FOCUS.* Figure out what you want and do everything you can to get there (while also being a good person). That's all it really comes down to in the end.

If you enjoyed reading this book, please go on Amazon and give it a rating and review.

I'd love to hear from you, and if you have any more questions or you feel that I've left something out feel free to connect with me on Facebook or by email.

-Ryan Sand

Made in the USA
Middletown, DE
18 May 2019